Thirty-Six

Other Books by the Author

Flying through Glass (poetry)
Traveler's Advisory (poetry)
Man with a Thousand Eyes and Other Stories (fiction)
Northwest Variety: Personal Essays by 14 Regional Authors
      (essays; co-editor)
Trolley Lives (poetry)
Caught in the Revolving Door (poetry)
Persnickety (poetry)
Nickelodeon (poetry)

To Wendi —
I loved your
singing / songs —
and sharing
the program.
Steve

THIRTY-SIX

poems

Steven Sher

A Donald S. Ellis Book

March 2, 2003

CREATIVE ARTS BOOK COMPANY
Berkeley • California

Thirty-Six is published by Donald S. Ellis
and distributed by Creative Arts Book Company.

For information contact:
Creative Arts Book Company
833 Bancroft Way
Berkeley, California 94710
1-800-848-7789

ISBN 0-88739-419-1
Library of Congress Catalog Number 99-XXX

Printed in the United States of America

Acknowledgments

The author wishes to thank the following publications, where poems from this collection first appeared, some in different form:

Calapooya Collage ("A Word To The Insomniacs" and "Resonance");
Chili Verde Review ("The Space That's Growing Small Around Us");
Clackamas Literary Review ("My Father's Cheek");
The Eloquent Embrella ("Miriam's Dream—Mileses, New York, 1992");
Fireweed ("At Dusk" and "Mastering Death");
Hubbub ("Soul In Flight");
Israel Horizons ("The Finger Of God");
Manzanita Quarterly ("A Time For Rain");
Mistry Guild ("Stones For My Mother");
Passager ("A Day Like This");
Pembroke Magazine ("Menorah");
Response ("After A Photograph Of The Old Jewish Cemetery Of Prague");
Skylark ("Return To Light");
Solo ("The Consecration Of The Priests");
Talus And Scree ("Out Of The Shadows" and "Pursuit");
To Topio ("Wind And Trees");
Witness ("The Awakening" and "The Box Of My Father's Clothes").
"The Box Of My Father's Clothes" later appeared in *Olam.*

Special thanks to Richard Fein, Tom Ferté, Glenna Luschei and Roger Weaver for their helpful comments and encouragement during the manuscript's completion.

*In blessed memory of my father,
Albert Sher, 1922-1991;
and for my teachers,
Menke Katz and John Ashbery*

Contents

III.

Introduction

Mirror and Ritual: The Poems of Steven Sher

Thirty-Six by Steven Sher refers to thirty-six righteous persons living in each generation, without whom the world wouldn't survive. Throughout these quiet, loving and humorous poems about a father, the reader comes to know why such a person ensures the survival of the generation. The book is filled with memories of comfort that make it especially meaningful to read in times of grief. It came to me at the time of my daughter's death as a deeply felt spiritual exploration.

In "The Consecration Of the Priests," the poet describes stubbing his toe during the last days with his father. A year later, as he commemorates the date of the death by lighting the candle which burns for the entire night and day, he feels the pain again. "This solemn promise: as I ache I will remember." The many turns and aches in this book flow towards healing. They helped me become well.

In another poem, "The Finger Of God," the poet imagines on the night of the second Seder he hears his father's voice singing:

> The door flies open. God helps him
> off with his pain like an overcoat
> a sick man can't remove himself.
> My father's parting songs—
> *Haggadah* of his blessed memory—
> his fragile voice, a gift
> he leaves the living.

When the poet (in "The Box Of My Father's Clothes") lifts up his father's old clothes to himself, he is at last encouraged to go forward:

> the child so quickly an adult,
> a man so quickly expired—

After spending a year with these poems, I realize how the firm, insistent tone has stayed with me.

> Black linen on the mirrors, first
> seven days, softened his death.
> (from "Soul In Flight")

The impressive fact in this book is that it is bound both by the startling image of the mirrors and by the softened ritual. To me as a Christian, these lines draw up what I perceive as the new Judaism, ritual being tradition and mirror being the inward looking reflection.

I think the reader will find, as I did, the urge to return to the book month by month, year to year.

Glenna Luschei
San Luis Obispo, California

Preface

I've no way of knowing whether my father was one of his generation's righteous thirty-six (*Lahmedvovniks*), whose presence ensures this world's survival. In Jewish legend, these "hidden saints" are unassuming and humble. All I know is that his good name is widely praised. And he's remembered for his generosity and his sacrifice for others.

Steven Sher
Corvallis, Oregon

Thirty-Six

I.

My Father's Cheek

for Roger Weaver

Near the end of my father's life, the hope
already melting in his eyes,
we hugged and held,
embraced in silence, knowing
there might never be another
chance, no touch again between us.

But on this mild night, like Florida
then, his departed soul
remembered goads a rush of air.
I feel his hand upon my back, the brush of
stubble of his beard, once more
his cheek against my cheek.

Florida, March 1991

Approaching the unthinkable, I have
flown into a suffocating heat that
soaks into the bones like worry.
At once I spot my mother among
the push of passengers. Beyond the gate
a frail man, the cap upon his head
too large, watches me like a child
with hopeful eyes. Slowly, his face
registers. Weeks of chemotherapy
have turned dad's tan glow pale yellow,
set his eyes ablaze. How quickly
years can dwindle to a trickle
of days. Love, running through us
like false hope, still tightly binds us,
twists of rope. Then silence,
as we hug, reminds us of the good
cry yet to come, a time when
death won't be unwelcome
and the dying upon their backs
carry humanity into the unknown.

The Consecration Of The Priests

> *And when it was slain, Moses took of the (ram's)*
> *blood thereof, and put it upon the tip of Aaron's*
> *right ear, and upon the thumb of his right hand,*
> *and upon the great toe of his right foot.*
> Leviticus VIII: 23 (Hertz-Soncino edition)

In the company of my father a final time,
I stubbed my toe, badly bruising it,
walking into a door of glass I didn't see.
One year later, the weather turning
damp, my big toe torments me again.

This solemn promise: as I ache I will
remember. I enter time as pure of heart
as the high priest setting foot
in the Holy Place, the great
toe throbbing with blood, walking on air.

Summoning prayer, I stand before
the *yahrtzeit* flame as I stood before
my father last, my weight upon
the one good foot, the moment
clear of fear and pain.

Flight

Beyond the blinking doubts,
above the far and separate towns,
we've come the whole dark
continent like wind
atop the backs of clouds.
As we descend in fog, our destination
bubbles up under the wing.
We circle, float, begin again
to trust what can't be seen, again
attempt to land. Impatient,
the plane like a fist
pokes a hole in the fog
and crosses quiet highways.
Now there's nothing left
to keep us out, not the glare
of lights or anything that moves
we might have startled, not our
anxiety about the world to come,
out there waiting in the night,
which sticks to us already
like dust along the way.

Mastering Death

Struggling through
this life we finally master
death the way
a child falling, always
falling, learns to walk.

Grown attached
to dark our days
like shadows stretch
the length of
road ahead.

Eternity shouts
for us, *Pick up
the pace.* Our souls
crazy to fly
sprout wings.

The Finger Of God

Passover, 1991

A cloud points, stretched
like a finger before the full moon.
The world, standing accused,
hides silently in shadow.
For now those dreams we chase
across the night will quickly fade.

We become, without strong faith,
more comfortable with our doubts
than in the company of false
hope, pulling up the blankets
to our necks against the chill
at dawn, the open window.

A faint sound rises above grief.
I hear my father, the night
of the second Seder, from Florida
where he went happily to revive
his life, singing as he sits
hunched on his bed, chin on his chest,
sinking in the other world.

The door flies open. God helps him
off with his pain like an overcoat
a sick man can't remove himself.
My father's parting songs—
Haggadah of his blessed memory—
his fragile voice, a gift
he leaves the living.

Return To Light

Breaths spilled from him
into the sheets, a fading
dream he fought to see
to its uncertain end.
Face up, he saw forever
across the hovering night.
So cold, it was so cold
as he was drifting free
of space and time, no longer
holding on to anything he knew.
What mattered most: he was
home in his own bed, while wife
and daughter and her future
husband, resilient as
the dawn, slept fitfully,
still dreaming of that
gradual return to light.

Somewhere In The World

The end of a life, in darkness
lost, like a falling tree
will make no sound when none
among the living hear it.

Morbid thoughts have crept
inside me, now exhaust me.
All I dare hope to do is sleep
and wake, the great nagging doubts

gone for good. Gone,
that shudder at the thought
of our becoming dust,
drifting through the universe.

Wherever we go, whatever form
we take, whatever darkness
beyond the darkness of this world
we inhabit—I close my eyes,

afraid as day slips into night,
my racing heart rejecting pain,
more alone without my father
being somewhere in the world.

After A Photograph Of The Old Jewish Cemetery of Prague

1.
Like a crowded mouth of teeth,
twelve deep, the headstones
blacken and decay.
This is no place to sink
one's tears. Scar upon scar
can scare the curious.

2.
I'm grateful for my father's grave
and the space beside it
waiting for my mother: nothing
save the quiet beneath a canopy
of stars, our parting tears,
like petals spread to pacify each step.

Soul In Flight

Ours is the story of the struggle
of the soul, where passions battle and divide
the years we live from the time we die
like two sides of a mind:
one side hopeful, the other stolen
to despair. The truth, a crack of air,
relentless cold, will rush to fill these rooms.

How I have run to feel the world
against my face and put new miles between
myself and my worst fears, longed
to feel the loving hand of motion on my face,
the stirring of the elements
that never seems to cease when we are young,
fends off the end of everything we know.

Now I wander with the river, pitch
flat stones, spot the traps the eddies
set, catching limbs and leaves;
study the muddy bottom as if a memory
will come unstuck. Still I believe in
happy ends, follow my heart into the calm
that follows flight, exile of silence.

The clouds never seem to tire of
their endless pursuit. I stand in awe
of that invisible push, the wind,
and how it snags what's in the way
and how things slither along
like the pulse in my wrist, these hands
driven mad with movement.

My father demanded peace when the simplest
motions and the slightest sounds
became too much for his frail frame.
"This is no life," he finally said
and shut the brain, then stopped
the heart and in a moment all
the world collapsed around him.

Black linen on the mirrors, first
seven days, softened his death.
We sat shoeless on hard wooden stools,
feeling what it was like not to have
our lives race forward, not to wash
the dark from our faces. Not knowing
where the world would rush back in.

Standing At Woodstock

April 1991, for Charley Gelish

The yearly pilgrimage begins
and through the summer faith
will build until some swear

they still can hear the thunder
of the crowd, see beyond
the years of doubt.

A generation stood together
on this open palm of earth
and glimpsed the future.

How fitting that my friend
whose family owns this land
has brought me here to walk

in silence, first day after
sitting *shivah* for my father,
first steps back into the world.

My heart, broken in half,
now folds like hands, the one
inside its mate consoled.

I recall how half a million
souls were lifted from
the mud, the flood of song.

Who came before and all to come—
forever linked, together
singing at this Sinai.

A Day Like This

It will be a day like this, our last
day in the world. All we possess
will be set free into the streets.
A quickening wind will stand us up,
undo how we are bent to move ahead,
and sun will flutter through
the trees. Our dreams will burn
like endless heaps of fallen leaves—
our memory like smoke adrift
in the six directions—until the last
breath slips away, until
the soul, eye of this storm,
is lifted in the circling dark.

II.

The Space That's Growing Small Around Us

Now when nothing that we hear
seems real and little of what
we see makes sense, the promise
of the world begins to close up
like harsh light shrunk to a pinhole
and yet, on the other side,
if we would only dare to look,
hope's blinding light is like
the back of God that Moses saw.

Everything beyond our reach
must surely make a difference.
People disappear from life
and it seems the dreary winters
come more quickly than before.

O that I and all I do could change
the way things are, could
hold the dark back with a glance,
disarm the world, or at the worst
prop up the saddened human spirit
with a shaft of light like a stick
holding up a box. But no one
can undo the trap, the dark
that waits to snare us soon.

O that we, these days of pain,
could find new faith, remake
the world so everything
that was on top is on the bottom
and on the bottom, on the top.

Menorah

for my uncle, Hank Sher

Once there were six
children, like lights
on a menorah, but one
by one by one they have
gone out until just one
remains, the youngest
son, and he grows weak.

Beside him, standing
in the window, is the light
of the next generation,
the light of living
memory, vigilant flame,
which keeps away the dark
of our forgetting.

Out Of The Shadows

The child in my daughter's bed
could be the frightened
boy, same age, who hid
when death lit from behind
by hallway light stood watching
with its wide eyes from
the darkest corner of the room.

How we, father like daughter,
react so much the same,
two minds cut loose
in death's confusion, about
to burst with cold sharp air,
the pain so new that none
can know what shadows hold.

Hallway Light

My pain grows dull, becomes a whisper
of the scream that it once was.

Still I want to scream when I think of
losing you. I want always to scream
to shake contentment from the world,

scream as sons were never taught
but only be the cause of others' screaming.

These months I dream I walk the hall
between my room and yours as I once did,

unable to sleep. A long-forgotten fear
of death returns. My shuddering soul
runs to the hallway's end where others fell

over the edge, where again you leave
a light through the night burning.

A Word To The Insomniacs

Wakefulness has much to do
with loneliness. Images of stolen
futures, smuggled frightened
from my dreams, float into the night.
Nothing to be done but endure
the pain, embrace this passion,
cold twisted sheets the only shield
between me and the dark.

My father at this early hour
sat reading his paper at the table,
preferring silence to his dreams;
bent each day like a shadow
moving through the rooms
at the same angle over the print
and pattern of his life.

We find new faith in silent
spaces, spun from shadow. Some
reject it out of hand, prefer
consuming light, pursue the crowd,
fill their lives with sound,
consoling chatter, as if
this alone will matter and
negate the end of days.

Miriam's Dream—Mileses, New York, 1992

for my mother

Tenderly we're rendered silent
by her silence and her stare
elsewhere, her vacant face
like the gaping hole in the old barn,
her spent strength like the weathered wood
that will collapse if our eyes
linger too long, eyes
that look too much like his.
In the distance, beyond concern, birds
settle on the sign for posted land.
Dinner done, we talk of hope for our souls.

But our worries mark us as these trees
and posts have marked this field,
sunk in quiet earth, apprehensive
dusk, the distance now deceptive.
Here tall grass creeps up on us,
its intentions unknown. Vulnerable
in the open field, our thoughts
are lost in clouds of dust the mind kicks up
at some imagined hum: a clearing
throat, unsettling cough. Those
who doubt have reason to believe.

She had lost all hope, but in a dream
a butterfly has touched her cheek.
Someone says, *Don't we live on?*
At once she flies after his question
the way the wind chases the rain
or the grass heaves to be free
of the earth, like spirit
from flesh, the way this world
will rise to meet the other one,
sun meeting dusk, pain meeting
peace, light meeting dark.

Resonance

My son curls on the carpet
as my father did to take a nap.
My daughter's raw emotion,
fed a portion of despair,
mimics my mother's loss.
My nervous motions were
determined by a thousand years
of frantic pacing, wringing hands.
Our short lives echo
others that have come before.
Our nights repeat the blink
of stars, the dead forever
smiling, rubbing eyes.

Remembering Thomashefsky

for my daughter, Kyla Morgit

Everything requires urgency,
from the wild eyebrows
and the wide-as-saucer eyes
to the slap of the hand
that emphasizes every point
upon the table or a thigh,
from the timely thought that
cannot wait to take its place among
the other thoughts tossed out in talk
to the *pish* which pleads
to be let out. We are a family
of fanfare and histrionics.

Thomashefsky understood
the stuff of modern melodrama,
that panic people feel
when dying over the slightest hurt,
a stubbed toe, blood rushing
to the lungs and not the wound,
or when hearing some heart-stopping
news, standing over a bowl
of peeled potatoes in the sink
like someone dying in his bed.
Our calls for help can split
a night like a skull in two.

Nothing in this day is calmly done. No
holding back accusing tears,
no stifling screams that
will unsettle even the calmest
combatant, the unsuspecting guest,
for there is no other option
but to scream, simply to be heard,
to hurl concerns against
the ceiling and the walls so everyone
can't help but know there is
in the world another loud
undaunted whirlwind loose.

The Nights He Cried

for my son, Ari Dovid

Down on the floor
he tumbles, fluttering
lips like a whinnying
horse, giddyap gone.
Missing grandpa
now he builds a wall of
tears around the pain—
the way he covers
someone at the beach
with sand, warning
the body being buried
not to move or it would
ruin everything. My
son discovering, safe
in my arms, how one
begins again to trust,
stuffed teddy crushed
against his chest.

Grandpa's Worry Dolls

You discover, rummaging
through the quiet rooms, the worry
dolls the children sent their
grandpa, to which he confessed
his final fears, placing them
under his pillow while he slept.

People stumble through the world
but to what end? What good is
made of what we do? Time
is fragile, the sentence harsh.
There is precious little,
once we vanish, left behind.

Bands of twenties, bankbooks,
bonds in housedress pockets,
jackets, slacks—in Florida
the old ones live as Jews
in Europe did, expecting always
to be robbed or leaving.

Parallel Lives

The space I occupy becomes a shadow
of what it was, a doubt
which quickly grows from
something sure and bright,
this passage into darkness.

Two vehicles have tried to run me off
the road, veering over the line
into my lane. And then,
rear-ended—third time
the charm—I'm sent into a spin.

I share, same age, my father's
fate: whiplash for me;
he, breaking his ribs.
It was a time he too began
to be invisible and slip away

without our noticing
for a quarter century more,
when age initially betrayed him,
when mortality provided
comfort for the pain.

Stones For My Mother

Brushing off the loose
dark earth, she lovingly holds

his memory like a stone
in the palm of her hand.

Where has the rock
in her life gone?

Smoothness of stone
steadies her hand,

some cold small comfort
found in every rub.

III.

The Forgiven

Who will remember, much less
care, that we lived as we did,
that we dreamt of a world
much better than this and yet
did nothing more than
dream, left nothing to the world
but an empty space where we
once stood, silence
where there could have been
a passionate shout, where
we forever turned away
from our forgiving fate?

The Source Of All Things

If sadness moans within your
bones, explore the source

of pain. Succumb to rage.
Swirls of hidden emotion

like the whistle of a train
already lure you to your end.

Like driftwood, restless
in this sea of days,

your dreams, sweeter than air,
float through the screens,

under the door. The soul
set free, your cry

ascends, a holy
spark ready to flame.

Return To Dust

Each drop of rain against
a face transforms a waking
moment in this life.
Soon the deluge is delivered,
emptying the past. Our greatest
fear fills lungs and floods
the Earth as memory
is shaken off the back of this
exhilarated beast. The sun
dries up the years like mud.
And dust which rises
in the wind repeats the dream.

Rainy Season

The earth turned green exerts
an unexpected calm. We grow
as tame as trees, whose thick
roots rarely reach the surface.

Listen, in the distance,
to the muffled cries: a sudden
downpour burning streets,
peeling sheets of flesh.

What sort of God invents
slow death and then,
without regret, boards up
the sunny windows to the world?

At Dusk

Shadow enters thought as we pursue it
to an end we cannot see, barely imagine.
Time unwinds like a ball of yarn
and we are never sure which end,
if we can find an end, is the beginning.
Our clutter of doubts, the wad of threatening
clouds stuck in the sun like a balled up
handkerchief, holds back the light
without it damaging our eyes.
This darkness suits us. Unlike
the vegetation which grows greedily
towards light, we grow towards dark,
gravitate to inner lives.
Soon darkness follows everywhere
we go. We add to it, turn houselights off.
Stumbling through the empty rooms
someone objects, "There will
be darkness soon enough."

Mother To Daughter

In a recurring dream my mother waits
for the night to cease, steam heat
and creaking floors to settle;
neck stiff, head raised from her pillow

for our safe arrival home.
In her memory, slick street
slow-going, her mother doesn't bother
fussing with the buttons on her coat.

By then the snow has swirled up
on the porch, covered the front stoop;
footprints leading in and out
like explanations for the worst of endings.

Her mother ducks from the wind
down blackened block toward the light.
Up a porch, calling her daughter's name—
but it's the wrong porch, next door

to where the girl sits for a neighbor.
Panicking as no one answers
grandma skids, landing on her hip
at the bottom of the steps.

This warning echoes, defying time,
instills an image of her limping
till the day she died, hiding
nothing of the pain others denied.

Pursuit

Death, like wind without pause,
pursues the moving target.
Maybe he'll be taken quickly—
a car wreck or a bullet
to the brain—and maybe not.

We turn the burning questions
on their heads for answers.
Next moment, an explosion
panics the soul and—poof,
he's gone. Oh God,

why him and not another?
For us the end of things
is too much grief
and yet, in the end,
no one can wait.

Wind And Trees

On hearing God in the howling
wind, we're moved to fly,
begin to sway like trees
stretching these desperate
days to unexpected years.

Worn slowly loose the weakest
topple, torn from clouds.
If only we owned trees' deep
roots. So quickly we are
blown beyond this world.

The Awakening

There's not a day I dread
but this getting out of bed, dead
of winter, the room so dark I can't
be sure my eyes are open
or whether the world predawn,
rain tapping like a dream
at the window, is really there.
I strain to see beyond the dark,
slowly blink away the night.
I could cry or throw a tantrum,
but nothing can speed the reassuring
light through slits in the blind.
Already screaming at the foot of
the bed, a litany of chores, impatient
children climbing in beside me
with their cold feet and their
hundred questions and the same worries
as when they went to sleep.
Nothing changes day to day:
turn up the heat to dry
the windows; straighten the sheets;
prepare something to eat. My body
becomes the obedient servant
once I propel it blindly
through the rooms, one direction
every dawn.
                    Have you ever
felt depressed by any of this—
the closed gray house, the rush
to leave it, the sameness
of your motions? Small wonder

our sages created morning prayer,
ritual a bit more difficult than
turning on the burner for a pot of tea,
to resuscitate the soul. And over
generations, sustained by sameness,
our every bow and every turn
and every muttered phrase,
dependable as breath, meant
our survival. Would death
be any better bed of roses?
You could expect there'd be
a certain amount of sameness to it,
just like life. Except
we wouldn't have to fuss with hair
or dig through drawers to find
a pair of matching socks. Perhaps
it's best not to have so many
distractions.
        Exhilaration,
as we grow old, at the prospect
of an everlasting soul,
boldly sustains us through
those final months of failing health,
renewed attention to old habits
we're reluctant to give up,
death's preliminary repetition.
Think of how the dark will
never bother us again. Nor will
the cold. And the early light that
streams in through a window,
the one day we can sleep in late,
will not disturb our peace.
Finally we will know such
freedom. But what of God?

No morning euphoria for the supreme
being. Imagine the headache
from all the human nightlong questions,
cosmic chatter, the wrestling
that goes on in dreams. Imagine
God's worry over this lonely
creation, humanity,
and the fear, the almighty
fear of everything there is
expanding, neverending, and monotony
of all, that mounting time.

Measuring What's Lost

There's no human way to measure
what's been lost had a man not died
but lived another day, another minute, another
gesture, had he taken one more breath,
extracted it like a solemn promise
from the depths of air.
No mind can comprehend what a moment
holds and yet we speak of the world
in should have beens or ought to be's,
as if something inevitable were denied.
Navigating this uncertain ground
like a sheet of ice beneath our feet,
we fill our lungs with hope
each brave step forward. Maybe we'll go on
with the air knocked out of us,
our spirit deflated, our fate decried.
Maybe we'll fall and won't get up again,
landed on our faces in the dark, exposed
bone matted with mud, the flesh
adhered to ice. Poor frozen
souls. And what of promise
unfulfilled, our forgotten dreams?
Consider the one who is killed
before his prime. As our sages said,
it's as if all unborn generations
died with him, the world were robbed
of its limitless potential
and this exponential loss, counted out
each treacherous step upon the stunted
earth, lay packed beneath our feet.

A Time For Rain

He makes the wind blow and the rain descend.
from the Jewish Prayer for Rain

When the dry conditions linger
and all the living, like tinder,
shrivel under sun's unblinking stare.
When the earth has baked
for weeks on end and cracks
show in its rough brown skin.

When the wind in fitful starts
and stops begins to swirl.
When hope is scattered like the dust
and dust has covered all
we see and touch until it blocks
the entrance to the soul.

When the mind is soaring
and our thoughts are climbing
one over the other like desperate
men trampling men deserting
the lost cause, flames abandoning
the spark from which they came.

When the heart at dusk has sunk
into despair so memory blows
in all directions, gathers openly
where light and dark like lovers
hold, never considering where
one begins and the other ends.

When emptiness begs to be filled,
the rain for which we pray
will come like a good cry
from a clear heart and we will linger
here another year, climbing
from the depths of our sadness.

Then we, begun again to trust
the world, can close our eyes
and face the sky and drink
our fill of tears from every cloud.

The Box Of My Father's Clothes

Reluctantly I hold them up
and swear before the mirror
I begin to look more like he did
each passing year. His clothes
cannot tell us apart. Carefully
I then extend one jacket's
empty sleeve into the air
the way someone might lead
another back into the world.
Down into the cool long arms
I reach, sleeve by sleeve,
pushing one hand then another
free beyond the open ends.
My claim, more durable than time.
I imagine, standing straight
and proud, how he might have felt
in this wool coat. The weight
of his arm now on my shoulders,
the weight of worry dusted
from my back, the past encouraging
the present to go forward
like a shy but willing child,
the child so quickly an adult,
a man so quickly expired—

his arms my arms
my arms his arms.

Nancy Sher

Steven Sher is the author of eight previous books. His poetry and prose have appeared in over 150 publications and anthologies. A native of Brooklyn, New York, he lives in Oregon with his wife and two children.